archipelago

john martone

samuddo / ocean
2012

The book's epigraph comes from Ven. Chanmyay
Sayadaw's *Talks on Meditation Given in the Blue Mountains*,
copyright © 2010. Mitsuhashi Takajo's words on page 69
of this book are drawn from Makoto Ueda's *Far Beyond
the Field*, copyright © 2003, Columbia University Press.

archipelago
copyright © 2012 by john martone
samuddo / ocean
ISBN 978-1-105-79416-2

archipelago

letterbox

cabin

little thought

sweet peas & sledge hammer

knuckle

laetoli

irises & velvet mite

archipelago

flowerpot kasina

tomorrow

shovel

a look

apostrophes (dew)

Unless the actions of the daily routine are performed slowly, the attention cannot precisely catch each individual movement. Only when you slow down all actions and movements in the daily routine, whatever it may be, can your mind catch each individual action and movement and realize its arising and passing away, its impermanence, and so on.

The Venerable Ananda himself attained arahantship by being aware of daily activities. …

—Ven. Chanmyay Sayadaw

letterbox

letterbox
a really big
letterbox

steel wool —
then paint

letterbox
bright black

rusted
steel

hand-me-
down

letter
box —
now it's

up
to you —

letter
box

close
as you'll

ever
get

to a
soul

it's
almost

time —
better

put up
yr

letter
box

in the time of the lord buddha…

drowsy —
wash
yr face

still
drowsy —

walk
into

the
water

go
deeper —

still
drowsy —

put wet
grass

on yr
head

you'll
get there

    (ajahn maha boowa)

dwelling
under
the trees

this is
a good
place for

exer
tion this
is what

the lord
tells us
to do

rain
barrels
al

ready
full
& it's

only
just
started!

cabin

mourning doves
mourning doves
what an odd dream

oak galls
& a human
cabin

floorboard
snug to floorboard
forest

pines candling
outside
pine walls

no heat
& no
toilet

forest
cabin

rags for
cleaning
cabin

good of them
leaving these
shelves empty

thin
as

can
be

one
brown

blan
ket

it's no
sourdough

mountain
lookout

look-in
cabin

sit down
in this
one chair
cabin

cabin
in a clearing
for now

a wind-
instrument
cabin

little thought

a world
washed clean
of words

a mind
washed clean

of words
a world

a mind
washed clean
of words

not of
this world

out of his mind — shepherd's purse in sun

sweet peas & sledge hammer

a sweet pea's tendril before you know it

good
morning

sledge
hammer

sledge hammer
& don't you know
shirt comes off

all those years
don't wear you down
sledge hammer

        sledge hammer
        all morning
        doesn't hear a thing

sledge hammer
you never
know when —

        this life
        lost to impatience
        sledge hammer

inch by inch
sweet pea
sledge hammer

those
climbing

genes —
chick pea
sweet

pea
roma
bean

human
spine

takes
you back
years

now —
      sweet
pea

keel
flower

*erector
spinae* —
sweet pea

trying
to get

back to
nature

concrete
rubble

this 12-
lb. maul
means it

way out here

    sledge hammer

        hydrogen atom

swings a sledge
hammer & his
glasses slip

breaking rocks
looking up —
shepherd's purse

it's
a time-
piece

    too

sledge
hammer

careful –

sledge
bounces
back

sledge
hammer

handle's
stem —

human
flower

pistil
or stamen —
sledge hammer

pinpoint
stars

sledge
hammer

back pocket work gloves

work gloves
thick as that
astronaut's

work gloves
closest you'll get
to angels

how you feel
work gloves
worn thru

stripped down to his work gloves

work gloves holding dirty hands

his work hat
in the stones
his accent

slaps that
work hat
on his knee

no sledge
hammer today

go plant
yr eggplants

everyone comes
from someplace else

w/ their own
vegetables

pea tendril
my eyes can't
catch hold

you always forget to latch the gate

knuckle

robin
swipes
a twig

while
you sweep

sweep
yr nest
clean

for birth
for death

one way
& the
other

frontal lobes
upside down
robin's nest

my thalamus
a garden
snail

from rat's
nest
to bird's

the end
of
his life

wren nest —
what dinosaur mansions!

planted pines
to make his house
disappear

you
forget
right

hand's
arthri
tis

when
the white

pine
candles

stained teeth
& his
shirt too

pissing —
see what's
inside

throat — wattles
where you're
going

lift
the cup

to yr
lips

that
is stone

soon there won't be
any more
mail

89 —
hands all one
knuckle

hip sockets —
never cross
yr legs again

laetoli

crush & smell
wild garlic leaf
these front steps

concrete broken
earth under
a thin moon

kitchen cabinets
trashed out back
the mysteries

under all this
concrete slab
all that earth

concrete pulled-up
roly-poly
rolls away

footprints under
a concrete slab —
laetoli

concrete slab cracks — my buddha

concrete
slab cracks —
those islands

push the
wheel
barrow

don't
look at
the

wheel
barrow

side-to-side
no no no —

empty
the wheel
barrow

wheelbarrow
rusting thru —
the wooden handles shine

a thousand dents
this wheelbarrow's
emptiness

no one's pushing a child in that wheelbarrow

it's the ungreased
wheelbarrow's
bird song

day's end & everything in a wheelbarrow

wheelbarrow a sermon on the void

irises & velvet mite

not
a pin
prick

velvet
mite

what goes on
in each of us
velvet mite

8
minutes

from
the sun

velvet
mite

somehow
fit 8 legs
velvet mite

velvet mite
still nowhere close
to zero

that's
a thought

velvet
mite

kicking a can
down the alley

such irises!

archipelago

*To write a haiku is to remove a scale. Doing so is
 proof that we are alive*
　　　　　　　　　　--Mitsuhashi Takajo

happy birthday —
it's the history
of an island

a small plane —
you're in the mud
planting stonecrop

patches of sedum
transplanted you watch
clouds move in

what
to name

this
island —

o
you won't

stay that
long

mourning dove
bottle-notes
off you go!

blowing across
bottle's rim
island music

floaters
in yr eye
those reefs

mother
is this the ocean
is this an island

no one
out there
an island

don't be
afraid

to let
go

it's
the life-
boat

    watching
            clouds pass
                      islands

sit still
for a cloud's
lifespan

cloud
  gone

just
  so

this body's an archipelago

snail shape
  thalamus
    washed ashore —

  aging
    body

  droplet
    of cloud

  ready
    to fall

  (& break
    that hip)

60 —
di
vided

by his
remain
ing

teeth —
impos
sible!

(eyedrops)

nightly

(island)

body's shape
eyedrop
bottle

clouds — islands —
scales on
his eyes

cataracts
soon you'll be
a tortoise

flowerpot kasina

5
billion

years
old clay

flower
pots

any number
clay flowerpots
extinct

one after another
setting flowerpots in rows
upside-down

glaucoma
& cataracts
clay flowerpots

washing
clay flowerpots
& two hands

10,000 years
gone by so fast
flowerpot shard

— uses a clay
flowerpot shard
to dig

clay flowerpots   each one the grail

a wasp nest
in this flowerpot's
empty too

a pair of mourning doves
among the flowerpots —
just listen

flowerpots
& beanpoles —
look at those stars!

you fill the smaller
flowerpots
before breakfast

sometimes going barefoot
among clay
flowerpots

clay flowerpots —
nevertheless
stepping in mud

it's a fractal world   clay flowerpots

a quiet rain
falling precisely
flowerpots

year after year
one flowerpot
comes back

one could
do worse than clay
flowerpots

      even w/out its bottom
      clay flowerpot
      flowering

           snail shell
           flowerpot —
           what were you thinking —

										clod

						the same floor has to be swept

				digging in shade
				you see all
				those roots

				puts that shovel
				aside to dig
				w/ his fingers

				digging in earth
				w/ his fingers
				out of the body

his fingers
in this earth
all of it

a fine day
a clod of dirt

clod of dirt
never knowing
how much life

clod of dirt
fingers come
out of nowhere

clods of dirt
& a whole
afternoon

clod
of dirt

heft
of an

inter
nal
organ

clod
of dirt
in

atten
dance

on the
sun —

tomorrow

more rain
house full of
cardboard boxes

electric fan
his room tonight
otherwise silent

one drawer
eyedrops &
ink bottle

cleans
his place
there's no tomorrow

all the same —
garden dirt
human dirt

scrubbing a floor
you hear those
wrens return

crow in that dead tree looks down on a garden

shovel

my
useful
life

my
shovel

another morning feels like the end of time

yr hominid instep
for pushing
a shovel blade home

yr shovel face
a shaman's mask
a journey down

shovel
the day

    blisters

shovel face
his own
toothless

shovel *face* –
breastplate –
fingernail

shovel what will you come to
shovel what you will come to

shovel where to throw it all

shovel yr body's 10,.000 muscles

shovel till it shatters on bedrock

listen
to yr

shovel —
each

time's
sibilant

shovel
the common man's
trapezius

shovel face slips thru the void between atoms

　　　　　　shovel
　　　　　　down —

　　　　　　(this
　　　　　　iron
　　　　　　age

　　　　　　is too
　　　　　　late)

you shovel yr way to a concave island

a look

a good spring day
to cart off those
old windows

they'll
never
make

double
hung

counter
weight

wood
window

sashes
in this

world
again

pulled out
that
window

an old
tooth
& felt

the space —
re
member

there's
no

*standard
size*

window
sash

yes — looking past
window's semi-

circle thumb-lock
at the moon

window glass too
ground-up
in garden

tongue
& groove
hand-

knotted
rope

&
5 lb
lead

plumbs all
gone
into

one torn-
out
window

gave
all his
day

to
window
sash

join
ery

once —
again

needing
rain

nothing but weeds that sunny spot

apostrophes (dew)

cliff swallows
surround you
having no home

river
flows gold
finches

oriole
redwing

starling
heron

canada
geese

all one
blessèd
way

when you wake up
dew is
another river

dew
on the ground
yr lesson

this side — that side —
dew's the first
membrane

anonymous as rising dew

dew
now mourning doves
take it up

a solar flare
comes to earth
in morning dew

dumb as
a rock
as dew

dew — must be
something to
disappear

dew the end of his night sweats

that bright
schoolbus
it's dew

the capillaries end in dew

not one
nucleus
dew

dew before & after the genome

taking notes
in the garden
dew

kingdom
phylum
class
order
family
genus
species
dew

www.ingramcontent.com/pod-product-compliance
Lightning Source LLC
Chambersburg PA
CBHW061450040426
42450CB00007B/1297